M000118988

57417881R00057

Made in the USA
Columbia, SC
08 May 2019